Internet Channel Marketing

Secrets for developing a framework for effectively using the marketing tools provided by the internet as a key component of your company's channel marketing strategies

By

Stephen C Campbell

© 2011 by **Stephen C Campbell**

Stephen C Campbell

ISBN: 978-1466480957

First Printing, 2011

Income & Liability Disclaimer

This document contains business strategies, marketing methods and other business advice that, regardless of my own results and experience, may not produce the same results (or any results) for you. I make absolutely no guarantee, expressed or implied, that by following the advice below you will make any money or improve current profits, as there are several factors and variables that come into play regarding any given business.

Primarily, results will depend on the nature of the product or business model, the conditions of the marketplace, the experience of the individual, and situations and elements that are beyond your control.

As with any business endeavor, you assume all risk related to investment and money based on your own discretion and at your own potential expense. By reading this document, you assume all risks associated with using the advice given below, with a full understanding that you, solely, are responsible for anything that may occur as a result of putting this information into action in any way, and regardless of your interpretation of the advice.

You further agree that our company cannot be held responsible in any way for the success or failure of your business as a result of the information presented below. It is your responsibility to conduct your own due diligence regarding the safe and successful operation of your business if you intend to apply any of our information in any way to your business operations.

Stephen C Campbell

Table of Contents

Preface

The term ***Internet Channel Marketing*** came into being during various conversations, radio presentations, training and consulting sessions with colleagues and clients in my attempts to appropriately define just where the internet is to be positioned in their eyes in terms of the business strategy development activities of the company that they were involved with.

With that in mind, allow me to draw your attention to the two main ways that I view the internet when related to business development.

1. In my view of the world the internet is to be viewed and managed as a marketing channel, to be used for promoting the business of the organization.

2. The internet is a channel that allows end user clients to consume and experience

the products and services that the company has to offer.

Other discussions led me to understand how confused many are when it comes to the use of Social Media Marketing and the use of all of the [other] available tools that the internet gives a business that it can use to interface with clients.

Corporate internet marketing strategy in line with social media marketing strategies seem to be at the centre of many of the questions that are posed to me; this is when business leaders are enquiring about the Internet Channel Marketing strategy consulting and seminar delivery framework which is the title and content of this publication.

The point is that many executives have been informed that they must get involved with Social Media Marketing, that they must immediately get training in this area, setup fan pages and profiles or else they along with their business will get left behind.

This is where I start to explain about the concept of …

Internet Channel Marketing

… or, how to effectively incorporate the marketing tools that the internet gives us into existing and new business strategies. Internet Channel Marketing is centred on the fact that the internet is but another channel to market. I say 'yet another with the thought in mind that it is a very powerful channel and should be fully exploited to reach out to end user clients.

As stated above in terms of how the internet is to be viewed for businesses we know that marketing channels are there to enable us to :-

* Effectively promote our products & services to current and potential end user clients

*   Effectively deliver our products and services to those who choose to purchase from us

Some of the more common marketing channels used for promotion and consumption are: -

- **Radio**
- Television
- **Newspapers**
- Department Stores
- **Yellow Pages**
- Billboards
- **Catalogues**
- Direct Mail
- **Niche Specific Magazines**

… so coming back to Internet Channel Marketing: I think it is important to highlight the fact that there are many tools within the complete internet marketing toolbox to enable

Internet Channel Marketing

us to accomplish our channel marketing objectives.

Internet Channel Marketing gives access to: -

- **Blogging**
- Podcasting
- **Social Media**
- Micro Blogging
- **Article Marketing**
- Forums
- **Directories**
- Joint Venture Marketing
- **Search Engine Marketing**
- Video Marketing
- **Affiliate Marketing**
- Online Press Releases

.... and the list could go on and on. Effectively using the internet for marketing means that we will use the combination of the above that adequately suits our business in terms of the..

 * Marketing category of our products and services

 * Market Segment of our target end user clients

… this may mean that we use mainly Blogging, Podcasting or Article Marketing or it may be the case that Social Media Marketing in line with Online Press Releases is used as a key part of our Channel Marketing Strategy.

That is the essence of Internet Channel Marketing where clients are instructed regarding the marketing tools available to them provided by the internet and; how to effectively use these tools to effect the execution of their business strategies.

It is with this last point in mind that in many cases I believe that it may not be the best advice to push companies and executives headlong into throwing money solely at Social Media as their (main) internet marketing push. To reinforce this point consider that it may be that the company's target market may be better suited to another more appropriate Internet Channel Marketing tool.

As I work with more and more clients on a global basis and deliver consulting in different industries, I have drawn from conversations with clients and attempted to provide high level relevant and useable information within this publication (from both a pure internet marketing perspective along with that of a more traditional marketing point of view) that can be applied immediately.

The techniques outlined herein are applicable for both B2B and B2C markets. This is important to highlight as many are still of the opinion that marketing on the internet is mostly applicable to B2C markets. The nature of B2C customers (frequent purchases, low priced ticket items, impulse buying, involvement from one or two people for decision making purposes) does make the internet an excellent vehicle for this market segment. For B2B purposes, perhaps (quality) lead generation moving onto guiding prospects through the marketing funnel (sales conversion) is at the top of agenda. Providing the sales team with leads who are interested in buying as well as those with an immediate need to buy is something that can readily be accomplished within the tools found within the Internet Channel Marketing framework.

All together it is hoped that the content will aid you in forging your business strategies whilst using the internet as a marketing channel to connect with your end users clients, engage with those who are to become your clients and to allow customers to experience your products and services in a manner that meets their needs.

The Internet Channel Marketing Strategy Framework

The Internet Channel Marketing core consulting process, strategy development framework and seminar delivery structure is based around a number of core modules as follows: -

INTERNET CHANNEL MARKETING PROCESS

The assumption is made that functioning organizations are already working towards a strategic business plan. It is the integration of this plan with the internet that can accelerate the desired outcomes.

For those (maybe smaller) organizations that are operating without a defined strategic marketing plan, it is advised that the following points are considered and relevant questions asked with the resultant output being used as input to the Internet Channel Marketing strategy.

- **Defined Target Market Segments**
- Key Decision Makers
- **Sales Cycle**
- Existing Marketing Channels

Understanding our *Marketing Segments* will give us a clear idea of exactly how and where to interface with prospects and clients in the online world. E.G. it may be more appropriate to interface with a particular market segment using Social Media; on the other hand we may come to the conclusion that White Papers may be the best way to get our information into the hands of the key decision makers.

The point regarding *Key Decision Makers* is an important one to make, as we need to understand at what point along the

Sales Cycle they become involved. The length of the sales cycle will shape the way that we output our information. Junior staff may 'touch our information first and so it is essential to make sure that they are engaged with (some sales cycles could take up to a year) up until the buying decision.

For added effectiveness we may wish to vary the Internet Sub Channels we use for communicating with different members of staff. Finally, respect needs to be paid to the existing (non internet) **Marketing Channels** that are being made use of. The internet sub channels may be used to interface with these Marketing Channels or used to supplement the activities being made through them.

Whatever decisions are made must be done from a strategic point of view; this is accomplished when considering the complete business strategy and integrating online marketing into that plan from a process management perspective.

INTERNET TERMINOLOGY GLOSSARY

This is where we do the leveling and go over some of the more technical internet related terms that managers and marketing professionals need to be conversant with in order to make informed decisions with respect to how to incorporate the internet into their marketing strategies. Some of the terms we talk about are Wikis, Social Networking, Blogging & Forums. The objective is not to turn the marketing professional into a technical whizz but to enable her to know enough to be able to competently meet the objective as stated above.

INTRODUCTION

It is here where we look at the global and local trends in terms of the use of the internet as it relates to your business. We look at trends such as the use of mobile devices & social networks with the thought in mind that your existing or potential clients could be interfacing with you there.

An example of this is based around my consulting work in China where tools such as Facebook, Twitter and Youtube are not available (at the time of writing) to allow companies to interface with clients. However China has its own set of tools such as: -

- **Renren (social networking platform similar to Facebook**
- Kaixin (another popular social networking site)
- **Pengyou (video sharing site similar to Youtube)**
- Youku (another video sharing site)
- **Seino Weibo (micro blogging site similar to Twitter)**

… meaning that the same principles and strategy execution steps made use of by western corporations can be used in China.

17

As stated earlier, the internet is to be viewed as a marketing channel and the growing global use of the internet is to be viewed by the business owner and marketing professional as an opportunity to use this conduit to build relationships that ultimately turn into revenue generation.

NEW MARKETING AND THE ORGANIZATION

In this section we look at how marketing has changed over the years; it has progressed from one of Interruption based marketing to where we are today with people largely engaging with us because they want to in the age of Permission based marketing.

To illustrate the point – when someone visits your company's website and signs up to receive information from you [in effect giving you permission to market to them], it is purely their choice whether to stay on the website or to go elsewhere to get that information. In contrast; an individual may be reading the daily newspaper where they essentially get interrupted by an advertisement for housing renovation material, clothes or to buy a new car. The advertiser has to skillfully divert [interrupt] their attention away from the initial [main] activity to get them to focus on something else.

Understanding how the organization will need to change in order to make a success out of using the marketing tools that the internet has given us is a critical point often overlooked by management. We have moved from where the core competence of the organization has shifted [is shifting] from manufacturing and distribution advantages to that where it is the sales and marketing activities that provide the core advantage.

The internet marketing tools of course allow us to broadcast our message faster and wider than ever before, the advantage and focus has moved to those who are more adaptable and have developed their strategies accordingly to align their core competencies with the use of the marketing and management tools that the internet brings.

OLD MARKETING AND NEW MEDIA MARKETING

In continuing to lay the foundation, a contrast is made between the old media marketing tools of limited channels which very much relied on interruption based marketing. This is contrasted with the expectations of how clients were (and are being) communicated with by using the chosen channels to deliver messages and products/services through to targeted segments.

Here it is important to embrace the fact that expectations have changed and current expectations are evolving rapidly. Of course, we know that the reasons for the modification in consumer behaviour is to a large extent due to how the internet has enabled consumers to communicate with each other and review the thoughts and opinions of other consumers on our products and services.

In addition to the above; company's are now able to conduct product research in ways that were not possible before, this in turn has a bearing on the ongoing development of the go to market strategies and in particular the speed of how we are able to gather data ready for implementation in the market place.

This ongoing strategy development has to be a careful blend of what worked in the past whilst taking full advantage of the marketing tools that the internet brings to the table.

REDEFINING THE MARKETING MIX

The marketing mix of course for many years has been the cornerstone of the development of numerous marketing strategies. The number of P's within the marketing mix is always up for debate but for the purpose of illustrating how the internet has impacted on this component of business strategy we will focus on the original four P's.

Product / Service: - Whatever it is that you happen to be delivering to the marketplace, it will be impacted in some shape or form by the accessibility of the internet and technology that today's end user has. There has been an increase in terms of the expectation of immediate accessibility of information and products; that of course has implications for the ongoing digitizing of products and services. This may be in the form of a straightforward ecommerce website option where clients can purchase products online, or a more sophisticated formula allowing clients to say design their kitchen with tools providing by your online business platform.

Whatever business you are in there is most likely a component of your offering that you are able to digitize and make available 24x7 online. This area of business development is working for many companies enabling them to forge ongoing relationships with potential and existing clients.

Some examples are the insurance companies that allow clients to choose different packages and services online at no extra cost prior to purchasing. We also have accountancy services that provide free online tax preparation services, clients often return for paid services after being engaged with the service provider and needing more in depth offerings. There are also implications for product development with the take-up of rapid 3d printing prototyping taking much of the expense and time out of traditional R&D modes of operation for various markets.

Price: - The internet gives businesses the opportunity to test prices online in various means such as geographically and even based on specific times of the day. Chosen product lines can be shown to clients from differing market segments at varying prices all designed to test user behaviour and to provide valuable data for in store purposes or for product line extension.

Innovative pricing models have had to be developed based on today's shortening product life cycles which in many cases rapidly leads to obsolete products. To deal with this, it is often difficult to publish and push fixed prices in hard copy and this is where the internet comes into its own enabling the organization to modify prices online based upon various parameters such as inventory, purchase location and price.

Customers can also be offered incentives such as coupons and discounts on products reaching the end of their life cycles, all this is only possible with the quality and real time nature of the information that can be provided by the organization to the marketplace with the setup of appropriate systems.

Experimentation can also be carried out with different online and offline prices, experiential pricing models can also be developed based on ongoing subscriptions as opposed to one off transactions. Free services and free trials along with the above can also be experimented with and incorporated into future strategy planning as appropriate.

Promotion: - I am of the opinion that all companies should be making use of the internet in addition to other means for promoting their business. The internet can be used as the main means of promoting a business or used appropriately to supplement existing methods of getting the message of the company out to the marketplace at large.

Promotion can be made using a multi channel marketing approach e.g. making use of offline means in order to drive customers online and using online methods to drive customers in store to make purchases.

Traditionally of course, end users had to respond to promotion activities by calling or writing for more information. Now, near immediate responses can be funneled back into the organization's ongoing marketing strategy development.

The internet enables global promotion in addition to options such as interactive advertising and the ability to showcase product options in a manner that has only been made possible by the use of the new technologies with the internet as the enabling factor.

Place: - Traditionally this has referred to channels of distribution which are of course used for getting our products and services into the hands of the end user customer. In the internet age customers expect to find products 24x7 wherever they may be located in the world. This provides the challenge for those global organizations to provide integrated supply chain systems to meet with customer demand.

It is down to the connectivity of today's world that gives us the ability to literally reach out to clients found in all corners of the world. Customers have developed expectations of immediate delivery and increased speed along with convenience such as being able to order and pay online and collect goods in store.

In conclusion – for future business strategy development activities it will prove useful to consider how the 4P's can be restructured for your business making use of the internet and the new technologies available to marketers and consumers alike.

NEW BREED OF CONSUMER

This component of the Internet Channel Marketing framework draws the marketing professional's attention to how today's consumer has changed in terms of mindset, expectations and consumption of products and services.

She has typically grown up with the internet and is very much used to consuming niche specific information with her buying decisions not being driven by yesterday's limited command and control broadcast marketing methods.

Instead the new breed of consumer connects with other consumers, researches the product that they are looking to purchase, listens to the opinions of others via social media and review sites and altogether are well informed when they come to make their purchasing decisions.

The implications for the business marketing community are enormous; there is a need to be a part of the conversation, to engage with potential clients early within the buying cycle that typically starts with an online search.

The implications and opportunities are for organizations to modify their lead generating strategies to fully embrace engaging with clients from an online perspective. The engagement is further defined by translating the demographics and psychographic market segmentation into internet marketing activities such as blogging, white papers and video marketing.

SEARCH ENGINE MARKETING

When a potential client lands on our website after performing an online search which is characterized by the keywords typed in to the search engine; this provides us with someone who has raised their hands as to the intention they have with respect to the products and services that we are selling into the marketplace.

This form of marketing is like no other form of marketing, it does not rely on having to interrupt the client in order to gain their attention and with surfers arriving on specific pages of our company website we have the opportunity to interact, answer questions (based on the search keywords) and provide them with the information they desire.

Having an understanding of the search phrases of potential clients enables the business to generate appropriate content (on social media sites, blogs, articles, forums, white papers, videos, press releases and other internet properties) on the internet, this content in turn containing specific references back to our main site aids in boosting natural Search Engine Results Pages (SERPs).

Paid advertising can also be used to drive clients to the main company website with pretty much immediate effect, however for long term internet domination and high SERPs; relevant content that is generated on a constant basis based on ongoing keyword research published on the internet with references (links) to our main company website lays a foundation for developing our strategies regarding using the internet as a marketing channel.

ENGAGING WITH CUSTOMERS VIA THE COMPANY'S WEBSITE

After executing the necessary tasks that will result in clients landing on our internet properties (this may be our corporate website, niche specific blogs, social media sites or even podcasting series) it is here that guiding (prospective) clients through a defined process in line with our business strategy comes into play.

The key point to emphasise is that it is here where the steps need to be taken in order to engage with customers in a permission based marketing method. For example, it may make sense to ask for the client's email address in exchange for providing them with certain pieces of information that they may be seeking from the company's product portfolio.

This is where interacting with clients online using as many modalities as possible (audio, video as well as simple text) gives us a better chance of entering into more of a dialogue as opposed to just delivering an information dump about what it is that we have to offer.

This is where customer segmentation really comes into play and understanding how to deal with users differently depending on which of our sites they arrive at and, how they happened to end up there (some of the methods used may include paid search, social media or through search engine marketing).

A good example of how to engage with clients is to look at the user experience one gets when visiting Amazon.com !! The point to bear in mind is that many organization's optimize their websites to enable users to search for information as opposed to encourage browsing and to help to answer questions that their users may have. This is where the use of blogging comes into its own with many companies setting up blogs specific to product lines that are separate from the main company website. The very nature of blogging encourages commenting and interaction; from here the opportunity presents itself for further interaction and leading clients through the sales process.

To be able to lead clients through the marketing funnel by definition implies that we will be implementing a lead generation program, customer contact details consisting of one or a combination of email address, landline number, mobile number, mailing address will need to be collected. This of course leads to the question – why would a person visiting our website want to give-up their contact details?

This is where one of the topics discussed in the Internet Channel Marketing framework of giving away products / services for free comes into play. The careful digitizing of something that is useful and desirable for the end user will enable us to exchange

33

contact details. The follow-up can be continued both online and offline.

Another point to note is that of bringing clients into the online marketing funnel after details have been collected in a more traditional manner of say – at a trade show, and; moving clients whose details have been collected online into the offline funnel – of say, direct mailings and phone calls. This multichannel method of moving clients from online to offline and offline to online serves to develop the customer experience whilst leading them through a defined process ultimately leading to more sales and revenues.

MOBILE MARKETING AND ADVERTISING

With just a brief look at the worldwide trends when it comes to the number of people using smart phones and internet enabled mobile computing devices; this channel of marketing looks set to become an increasingly key component when developing go to market strategies. The challenge of course is to incorporate mobile marketing & advertising into existing strategies when considering the necessary business development customer engagement outbound activities.

Text messaging, the use of QR Codes, game advertizing as well as appropriate email messaging are some of the tactics that can be used when adding mobile into the marketing mix.

The other side of mobile marketing is that of the user experience when viewing our business or corporate website on their mobile internet enabled device. From a business strategy perspective this raises the importance of considering the rising number of internet enabled mobile device users that may end up visiting our website and; the corresponding experience that will be given. Developing mobile friendly websites has forced itself into the business development discussions on a par with outbound marketing activities.

Developing an appropriate trimmed down menu of options for the organization's mobile website is something that should be high on the strategic marketing discussions with a defined plan to guide clients through the marketing funnel; this could be through offline activities or continued after pursuing the dialogue via the main company website.

Finally, consider that according to some projections, mobile internet usage will overtake desktop usage before 2015 (March 2011: Mashable); this of course has enormous implications for the ongoing marketing activities for organizations throughout the world.

SOCIAL MEDIA MARKETING

In line with our discussions on mobile marketing and advertising, it is of vital importance to consider that an estimated 91% of mobile internet access is for the purpose of socializing, contrast this with 79% on desktops (March 2011: Mashable). This serves to further illustrate the point of importance that mobile friendly websites have to play in the marketing mix. If we choose to use social media sites to advertise to our target audience; at some point in time they will most likely visit our main website whilst using their mobile device – mobile friendly websites have a part to play in guiding clients through the marketing funnel.

As this is all about using the internet as a key component of the business' marketing strategy; it is important to draw the distinction between social media marketing and that of search engine marketing.

With reference to the search engine marketing discussions above, we know that the keywords that users type into the search engines give us their intent (browsing for information, researching or looking to purchase) as they arrive at a web page on our website. As individual pages will be structured and optimized accordingly we can then act accordingly based on their intent.

Users on social media sites give their profile details when signing up and these parameters can be used to advertise as they come to socialize !! Note the distinction, search engine users come to our site with intent, social media targets have to be diverted from their main reasons for going to the portal.

Advertising parameters such as age, gender, marital status, having children (yes or no), associations, likes, languages, dislikes, home town, current living location and a whole host of others can be used to trigger the display of our advertisements.

The advertisement types that are available are numerous, some are: - banner ads, newsletter subscription ads, corporate profiles with fans and logos, get widgets and sponsored content. Different advertisements of course are more suited to targeted market segments.

In general; for social networking sites we have two methods for getting our target market to see our messages – CPM or CPC.

CPC – this form of delivering your message is based on the bidding of keywords or keyword phrases relevant to your target market segment, you are only charged each time a user clicks on your ad. This is an important point to note because as you only pay when a user clicks, you are able to gauge how 'clickable' or appealing your advertisement is. When they click, they are then redirected to your website, social networking page or elsewhere on the internet.

Using *CPM* (Cost Per Mille, or Cost Per Thousand), you pay per thousand 'impressions' (that is the number of times your ad appears online). Therefore, if your CPM is $5.00, the cost per impression is $0.005. The question arises, how do you know if someone has actually taken the time to view your message? The answer is that you do not. Your message will be displayed based on the parameters that you chose triggering the display – choose carefully.

Whether you should choose CPC or CPM completely depends on your goal, this is of course where strategy development comes into play! This of course is the main theme of the Internet Channel Marketing framework, to instruct and to encourage strategy development prior to targeted use of specific internet marketing tools.

BUSINESS TO BUSINESS INTERNET MARKETING

Along with the confusion that exists when it comes to the use of social media for the company's online marketing strategy development; there is skepticism and misunderstanding in existence when it comes to the part that the internet has to play in the role of B2B marketing.

Internet Channel Marketing

The question is whether or not the internet can be used to effectively guide the B2B purchaser through the sales process for more complex products that often have long buying decision making processes and high ticket sales. The ultimate purpose of B2B marketing is to assist the sales force to – well, sell! This is achieved through effective two-way communication with the target market.

After trust has been developed between the two parties, the company is able to articulate the desired outcome that the client is looking for. This will be framed of course in terms of that which is being sold. This principle does not change because we are using the internet!

B2B customers are using the internet for information gathering (based on the shift towards self education) and will gather information about our offerings from sources far beyond what we are able to offer on our company website alone. With this in mind they often have as much (if not more) knowledge than our sales people. The search for knowledge outside of our company's domain presents us with the opportunity to forge relationships with current and prospective clients throughout the various stages of the sales process.

B2B customers are *going to buy* and looking to buy as indicated by their intent in searching for and consumption of information relating to our products and services. With analytics and various tracking tools we are able to measure how much of and what content is being consumed. As we will be involved in the creation of the content, we can take the tracking information and use it to engage with clients offline as necessary or to guide and direct them through to the eventual desired sale.

Some of the Internet Channel Marketing strategy steps to focus on are: -

Focus on education rather than using hard selling; this is to be used with the ongoing creation of quality content, which focuses on the solutions that are delivered by your organizations products/services.

Create and foster communication opportunities that both educate prospects and place your company in a favourable light. Developing reasons for exchanging high value ideas and information using extranets, forums, blogs, videos, podcasts, articles and other options made possible by the internet serves to build the trust, which is necessary in B2B marketing.

Use email marketing, which gives clients a way to obtain additional information about our products and services. This allows us to stay top of mind and gives the experts within your organization an opportunity to publish their information in a structured format for consumption by clients.

Webinars that focus on the key concerns that are facing your clients (that can be addressed with your products and services) are a powerful marketing tool. As well as addressing the prospects live during the webinar; you should consider using the recordings strategically by placing them in multiple locations (your corporate site, syndication sites, niche blogs, forums, video sites).

Webinars and online presentations give users a different option for consuming our content and opting to come into our marketing funnel. The quality content will be recommended to peers and picked up by the media; a higher level of response is normally seen when colleagues of the decision makers direct them to consume your content.

The internet is a wonderful vehicle for B2B marketing; the reasoning behind this statement is that with all marketing we have no way of telling its effectiveness until someone has responded to our marketing content. One of the main differences between online and offline marketing is that in the online world we certainly have more visibility into how our target market is responding to our messages.

We can actually know who we are engaging with; in addition to this we can learn what is being said about our company, products and services. This can be determined (with appropriate tracking) whether a third party has received our message and acted upon it as well as if the action was taken by the person whom the message was sent to in the first place.

B2B marketing using the Internet Channel Marketing framework does require a different way of thinking than with traditional interruption based marketing, using some of the concepts within this publication will help your organization forge relationships, sell more and increase revenues.

CASE STUDIES

Various cases studies are used to both reinforce the key Internet Channel Marketing fundamentals and to show some specific instances of where companies use the internet channels for marketing and branding purposes. We also show how the internet is used to raise sales awareness and for real time service recovery purposes. Some of the cases considered are …

Blogging

This is widely used for many purposes in the internet enabled age which we live, blogging can also be used for business marketing. The smallest companies to the large corporates are making use of blogging, a framework for using blogs to connect with customers is highlighted with instructions for how your company can start to use blogs as a part of its marketing today.

Due to the nature of blogging and some of the legal constraints connected to the published content on a business website; consider the potential impact on a business of setting up a niche specific blog (say about ball bearings, designer watches or maybe test and measurement equipment) outside of the company's website domain. This will allow frequent updating of the content (with no potential legal implications for the company); and allow connection with those in the blogosphere who want to engage in discussions about our products and services.

Depending on the length of the sales cycle and; the nature of the discussions in line with the details and information about our offerings we can then choose to take the clients offline, direct them to our corporate website or any combination that is most appropriate.

Without going into too much technical details, it is important to note that the dynamic nature of blogging websites makes connecting with other internet properties more accessible, we can make use of pinging, dynamic linking, blog commenting, trackbacks and a whole host of features that blogging platforms such as Wordpress provides. Organizations are making use of simple blogs to drive multi 10s of $1000s of sales. Techniques for this are discussed during the Internet Channel Marketing sessions.

Free Business Models

These are prevalent today as a result of developments resulting in remarkable increases in micro processing power, internet bandwidth with the widespread usage of broadband along with increasing data storage capacities and the corresponding ease of access due to lowering prices. These three factors serve to turn past/current production parameters based on economics of scarce resources on its head. Traditionally, as resources are consumed, they become more expensive to produce; in the internet economy however it costs no more to deliver 1 unit of resource as it does to supply 10000. Digitizing products and services and using these within the business strategy are something for consideration. Consider how companies give away: -

- ➢ software and sell hardware
- ➢ (basic) accounting services and sell more complex service offerings
- ➢ search and sell advertising
- ➢ online games and charge subscription for more advanced gaming experiences

The point to consider is, how can your organization make use of this business model of giving away products/services for free in order to bring clients into the marketing funnel.

Content Leveraging

As the internet is essentially made up of content, your organization will essentially own more of the internet based on the quantity of relevant, quality online published content related to its products and services. Published content essentially serves two purposes:

1) To provide users with the information they are looking for in various formats such as video, audio and text. This of course should ultimately lead to assisting them with making a buying decision.

2) The content relates to search engine marketing as keyword relevant links within articles, blog posts, press releases, white papers and other content referring back to our main corporate website when spidered by the search engines will help to boost our rankings. This last point is discussed more in the section on search engine marketing.

Content creation on a consistent basis has become an essential component of effectively building ones brand and marketing on the internet. The fresh and topical content as we have stated earlier can contain keyword specific links which ideally should reference product pages, corporate websites, product social media pages and other company related material.

The repurposing of content means that one piece of content is reproduced in varying formats. For example – a 300-word article can be read and recorded and used as a podcast.

PowerPoint or Keynote presentations can be used along with the associated podcast to produce short videos. The original articles can be rewritten into the format of a press release. These are a few of the ways of repurposing and stretching our content out over the internet. Each format of content will be distributed via its own channel (podcast directory, video sites, news press release sites, blogs etc) on the internet all designed to build our brand and attract customers into our marketing funnel.

Micro blogging

This has been used for connecting with clients and to assist with real-time service recovery issues. In discussing making use of this form of marketing one point worthy of stressing is that this channel of marketing on the internet has been used effectively as an engagement channel – this is as opposed to a marketing channel of pushing messages out to clients.

Micro blogging sites such as Twitter and Sina Weibo (a major Chinese micro blogging site) in line with our discussions in social media marketing are places where people usually congregate for social purposes. This is where the stressing of permission based marketing needs to be revisited. When using micro blogging for connecting with existing and potential clients; note that users' attention will have to be diverted away from socializing to interacting with a company representative.

It is also worth noting that for this form of marketing to be successful; there will need to be support from within the organization. That is, not just from the marketing department but from other stakeholders from the other functions of the business.

Many organizations are making use of micro blogging by monitoring specific company related search phrases, responding to client conversations and building relationships. Used as a component of a company's strategy this method of marketing using the internet can lead to increased customer satisfaction leading to revenue generation.

Social Media Marketing

As mentioned above there is a specific distinction between social media marketing and that of search engine marketing. Having a firm grasp of the differences is an important factor when it comes to implementing marketing strategies using this form of media.

During the Internet Channel Marketing seminar we go into detail of how a multi $B organization makes use of social media for new product introduction purposes. Tapping into the power of the interaction of the subscribers of social media networks works due to the fact that word of mouth marketing along with peer recommendations are viewed at a higher credibility level than print media and online advertising.

The nature of social media marketing is very powerful and incorporating this method of connecting with clients into your marketing mix brings various benefits including …

- **Building relationships**
- Understanding how to improve customer satisfaction
- **The sharing of expertise**

Social media is a marketing channel that can be used to connect with decision makers and purchasers. You have the opportunity to start to attract more qualified prospects. Take a look at what social media can do for your business today.

Summarising Thoughts

Using the internet as a core component of your organization's go to market strategy for both B2B and B2C purposes can take your business to the next level.

B2B marketers can use this channel to engage with prospects at different stages throughout the sales process; at each step the opportunity exists for creating trusted relationships even before a face to face meeting ever takes place.

For those focused on the B2C market the ability to provide customers with that which they wish to purchase immediately exists.

Marketing using the internet means much more than commissioning someone in your organization to take charge of developing a pleasing to the eye website. Promoting the acquisition of customers via the internet to the boardroom by definition means taking an Internet Channel Marketing approach. I wish

57

you all the success as you embrace this wonderful mechanism for engaging with clients and ultimately increasing revenues.

About the Author

Stephen C Campbell has conducted business extensively throughout Europe, the Far East & the United States and is an expert at helping businesses of all sizes gain a dominant position in their defined marketplace through the integration of online and offline mechanisms.

Stephen holds MSc and MBA degrees & is a Master NLP Practitioner.

If you're serious about improving your own business' bottom line, and would like to schedule a consultation [Stephen is available to work with you face to face wherever you are in the world] to see how Stephen can work with you in the development of your marketing strategy, you can contact him by leaving your name, telephone and email address at

- http://www.StephenCCampbell.com

or by leaving a voicemail at

- 0044-208-123-8061

59